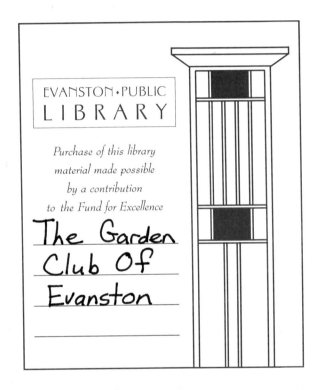

A Life Science Wonder Book

I Wonder What It's Like to Be an Ant

Erin M. Hovanec

The Rosen Publishing Group's
PowerKids Press™
New York

To Chris, my other favorite brother. Lots of luck and joy in things to come.

Published in 2000 by The Rosen Publishing Group, Inc.
29 East 21st Street, New York, NY 10010

Copyright © 2000 by The Rosen Publishing Group, Inc.

Photo Credits: p. 4 © CORBIS; p. 5 © FPG/Bill Losh; p. 7 © Animals, Animals/E.R. Degginger; p. 8 © Hans Pfletschinger/Peter Arnold, Inc.; p. 11 © CORBIS; p.12 © Minden Pictures/Mark W. Moffett; p.15 © Hans Pfletschinger/Peter Arnold, Inc., © CORBIS; p.16 © Animals, Animals/Joe McDonald; p. 17 © CORBIS; p.19 © Animals, Animals/Raymond A. Mendez; p.20 © Hans Pfletschinger/Peter Arnold, Inc., © Animals, Animals/Raymond A. Mendez; p. 22 © Minden Pictures/Mark W. Moffett.

Photo Illustrations by Thaddeus Harden

First Edition

Book Design: Felicity Erwin

Hovanec, Erin M.
    I wonder what it's like to be an ant / by Erin Hovanec.
        p.   cm. — (The Life science wonder series)
    Includes index.
    Summary: Explores the body, life, and environment of the ant and its importance in nature.
    ISBN 0-8239-5449-8
    1. Ants Juvenile literature. [1. Ants.] I. Title. II. Series: Hovanec, Erin M. Life science wonder series.
    QL568.F7H65   1999
    595.79'6—dc21
                                                                        99-29650
                                                                        CIP

Manufactured in the United States of America

Contents

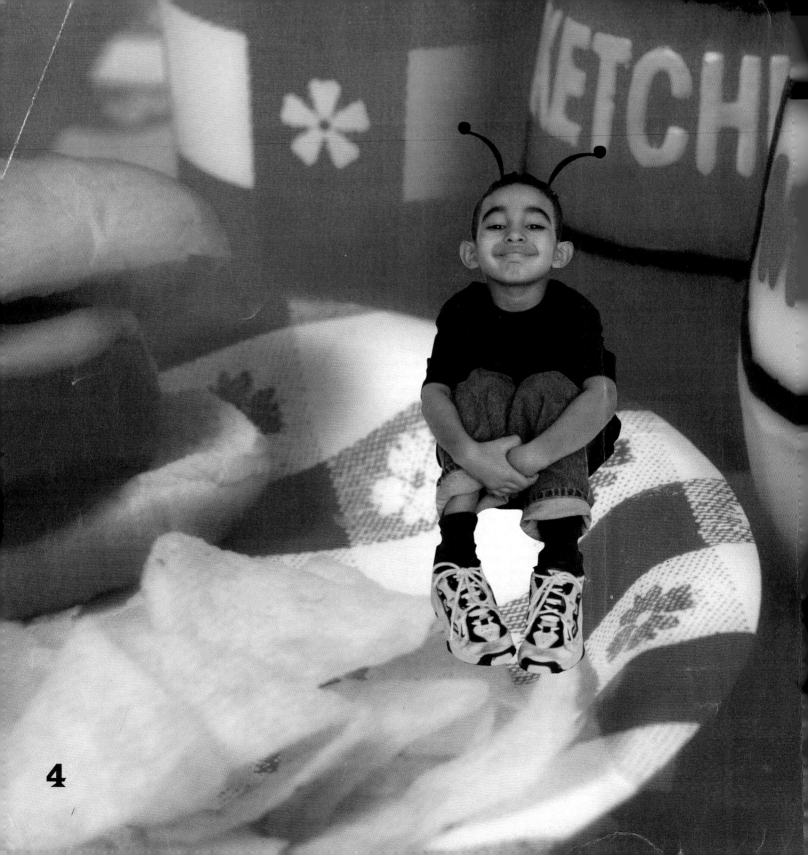

Awesome Ants

Imagine seeing a sandwich that's as big as a house, or a cupcake that's as big as a tree. That's what it's like for an ant when you have a picnic. No wonder ants are so eager to get in on the action!

Ants work very hard so they're often hungry. The biggest ants are over an inch long, which is bigger than a quarter. Most ants are very small, though. Some are so small that you can't even see them! Even though they're small, ants can do big things. Have you ever wondered what it's like to be an ant?

◀ *Your picnics are pretty exciting for an ant.*

Ant Antennae

Ant heads are very different from human heads. Ants have **antennae**, or feelers, that can help them find food, find their way, or even find their friends. Also, ants have two sets of jaws. They use their outer jaws to carry things, build **nests**, and fight **enemies**. They use their inner jaws to chew food. An ant's jaws move from side to side instead of up and down. What if your jaw moved from side to side? It would be much easier to chew with your mouth closed.

Ants' bodies also have six legs. Each leg has a claw at the end of it. Ants use these claws to help them climb and dig. Some ants have a pair of wings, too. Where would you go if you had wings?

This is a harvester ant. Like all ants, harvester ants have six legs. Each leg has a claw at the end for digging. ▶

7

8

Ants at Home

What would it be like to live three stories below the ground? It would probably be very dark and quiet. Sound scary? If you were an ant, you'd be right at home. Most ants live in nests that they build underground. Some nests are no bigger than your finger. These nests can have as few as 10 or 20 ants. Other nests can go 40 feet deep in the ground. As many as 10 million ants can live in a large nest.

Ants spend a lot of time building their homes. They dig tunnels and rooms using their claws. Sometimes these underground tunnels are covered with a pile of soil. These piles are what we call anthills, and they are there to protect the ants' nests. The tunnels can sometimes cover an area bigger than a swimming pool, and the piles of soil can be more than three feet high. That's probably as tall as you!

◀ *This is an anthill built by a community of red ants.*

Ants at Work

Ants are good **citizens**. They always look out for one another and try to do what's best for their **colony**, or **community**. That's because they are **social insects**. Social insects can only survive by acting for the good of their colony instead of for their own good. Each ant has a job that's important to the rest of the colony.

The **queen** is a female ant. She **mates** with the male ants to create young ants. Some colonies have only one queen. Others have thousands. A queen ant can live from 10 to 20 years. The male ants' only job is to mate with the queen. They have an easy life, but they live only for a few weeks or months. Worker ants are female ants who build and repair the nest and feed the young ants. The biggest workers are soldiers, who bravely defend the nest from enemies.

Worker ants usually live between ▶ one and five years.

11

Ants and Plants

Most ants only eat plants and seeds. Harvester ants collect seeds and store them in their nests. Some ants also eat flowers, fruits, and **insects**. **Fungus**-growing ants are very good gardeners. They keep gardens in their nests. In their gardens, they raise plants called **fungi**, which they eat. Honeypot ants eat a sugary liquid called honeydew. They gather it from plants (and sometimes other insects) and store it in their nests.

Ants also help farmers. They move, loosen, and mix the soil as they build their nests. This makes it easier for the farmers to plant their crops in the soil. The looser soil also helps crops grow better.

◀ *These ants are called leaf-cutter ants. In this picture, they are bringing leaves to their nest.*

Eating Insects

Eating insects may not sound good to you, but many ants don't seem to mind. Army ants hunt in large groups to catch spiders and other insects. Slave-making ants eat insects, too. They attack other ants' nests, kidnap their young, and eat them or use them as slaves. When the young slave ants grow up, their job is to find food and feed the slave-making ants. Some ants eat insects that would otherwise eat or kill farmers' crops. Ants that eat insects are called **predators**. Predators are animals that live by eating or attacking other animals.

Some ants, called dairying ants, get honeydew from insects like tiny **aphids**, who like to eat plants. Dairying ants stroke the aphids with their antennae until they give off a drop of honeydew.

Some ants are predators. Others, like the dairying ants pictured here, live off other insects, but don't eat them. ▶

An ant carrying a beetle.

Dairying ants and aphids.

Ant being preyed on by a wasp.

15

Staying Safe

Frogs are predators.

How would it feel to know that you could end up as someone else's dinner? Ants feel this way all the time. Ants are **prey** to, or food for, lots of animals, like anteaters, birds, frogs, other insects, lizards, spiders, and toads. Ants from one colony sometimes even prey on ants from another colony.

Some ants protect themselves from enemies by biting with their strong jaws. Sometimes they will gang up on a predator. A group of these ants will hold a predator still while others bite it. Other ants protect themselves by stinging their attackers with a painful poison. The poison is often thick and sticky and can make it hard for the predator to move. Some ants sting people when they feel scared or in danger. Even though they're so small, bulldog ants and fire ants have stings powerful enough to hurt a human being.

◀ *Ants are prey to many animals, such as the giant anteater, pictured here.*

Spreading the Word

How would you tell people things if you couldn't talk? Would you be able to get your message across? Since they can't talk, some ants tap on the outside of the nest when they discover food or an enemy. By tapping, they wake the ants inside the nest. Other ants have an **organ** that can make buzzing or squeaking sounds to wake their colony.

Many ants give off scents called **pheromones**. Pheromones give information to other ants through smell or taste. Ants use different kinds of pheromones to say different things. One pheromone leads ants to food. Another warns them that their nest is in danger. Ants also use pheromones to tell the difference between ants from their own nest and enemy ants.

Believe it or not, these two ants are talking. ▶
One is asking the other for water!

19

This queen is raiding another ant's nest.

Dangerous Ants

Could you lift a car all by yourself? Ants can lift objects 50 times heavier than themselves. Ants may be tiny, but they're powerful. Ants can also be very dangerous. They can even hurt animals and humans. Army ants attack by **swarming** in large numbers. A large swarm of army ants can eat a small animal or painfully bite a person. Some people are allergic to ant bites and have to see a doctor if they are bitten.

Tiny black ants can move into houses and it can be very hard to get rid of them. Carpenter ants dig nests in wood. These ants can destroy wooden buildings over time by eating away at them.

◀ *This strong ant is carrying a caterpillar that is very heavy. The caterpillar weighs more than the ant does!*

An Ant's Life

Ants have existed for over 100 million years. Humans have only been around for four million! There are over 20,000 different **species** of ants. They can be black, brown, red, green, yellow, or purple. Ants have antennae, claws, and wings. They dig underground tunnels, build huge nests, and have the power to lift heavy objects. It might be fun to be an ant.

Glossary

antennae (an-TEH-nee) Feelers located on an insect's head.

aphids (AY-fids) Very small insects that live by sucking juices from plants.

citizens (SIH-tih-zenz) Residents of a community.

colony (KAH-luh-nee) A community of ants that share the same nest.

community (kuh-MYOO-nih-tee) A group of living things in any one place.

enemies (EH-nuh-meez) People or things that can harm you.

fungus (FUN-gus) A plant, such as a mushroom, that has no leaves, flowers, or green coloring, and cannot make its own food.

fungi (FUN-gy) The plural of fungus.

insects (IN-sekts) Small, six-legged animals, such as ants.

mate (MAYT) When a male and female join in a special way to produce babies.

nests (NESTS) Homes that ants build, often underground.

organ (OR-gin) A part of a plant or animal that performs a certain function.

pheromones (FAIR-uh-mohnz) Special scents that ants use to communicate with each other.

predators (PREH-da-terz) Animals that live by eating or attacking other animals.

prey (PRAY) An animal that is eaten or attacked by other animals.

queen (KWEEN) A female ant that produces babies.

social insects (SOH-shul IN-sekts) Insects that live and work together in groups.

species (SPEE-sheez) A category of animals that have many things in common.

swarming (SWORM-ing) When a large group of insects travel together.

Index

Web Sites:

You can learn more about what it would be like to be an ant on the Internet. Check out this Web site:
http://members.aol.com/dinarda/ant/